The Ideological Foundations of the City-Building Tendency

The Ideological Foundations of the City-Building Tendency

By Caleb T. Maupin

Copyright © 2022 by Caleb Maupin

Dedicated to educating and fostering visions for a future beyond capitalism

All rights reserved. No part of this publication may be reproduced, stored in a retrieval system, or transmitted, in any form or by any means, electronic, mechanical, photocopying, recording, or otherwise, without the prior written permission of Caleb Maupin.

Contents

We Are the City-Building Tendency 1

The Masses Are the Water:
Understanding the Failure of Late-Marcyism 21

The sun of capitalism is setting; the sun of socialism is rising.

It is our duty to build the new nation and the free republic.

We need industrial and social builders.

We Socialists are the builders of the beautiful world that is to be.

— Eugene Debs, 1918

We are the City-Building Tendency

This article originally appeared in Platypus Review 142, December 2021/January 2022.

Since the 2008–09 financial meltdown, interest in socialism, communism, anarchism, and various anti-capitalist theories have been widespread among the U.S. public. However, this has not manifested itself in a revival of the labor movement or the enactment of social-democratic reforms. Austerity and the march toward a low-wage police state have continued. Regime-change wars and interventions by the Pentagon have continued with even less organized resistance than prior to the financial crash.

The various Marxist–Leninist sects, whose leadership are veterans of the 1960s and 70s political upsurge, remain more isolated than ever. While vague social-democratic concepts about "free healthcare" and "tax the rich" may be more popular today, knowledge of actual Marxist theory is noticeably absent. In this context, feelings of opposition to the status quo, the declining economic situation, the wars and out of touch elected officials have been hijacked by the Right wing. "Populism" is considered to be the property of right-wing nationalists, while "Marxism" is the label put on postmodernists and social-justice theoreticians emerging from the Ivy League schools.

Any serious socialist should be disturbed by this situation, and I certainly have been for a number of years. The biggest awakening came in Zuccotti Park on October 20, 2011, the day the gruesome death of Moammar Gaddafi took place. As an activist in the park, I noticed a big gap among the Occupy Wall Street activists. The seasoned left-wing activists, the Trotskyites, the NGO liberals, and the hipster trust-fund anarchists seemed to view the destruction of Libya in an almost positive light, as a "revolution" against a "dictator" who had "violated human rights."

But among the midwestern, working-class youth, many of whom had come to NYC with almost nothing, there were very different sentiments. Though these youth were ideologically not left-wing, attracted to a mishmash of libertarianism, pseudo-anarchism and conspiracy theories, they viewed Gaddafi in a positive light. They praised Gaddafi's efforts to build up an independent African currency, to build the African Union, and to oppose the U.S. war machine around the world.

Ideological Foundations of City-Building

Karl Marx and Frederich Engels put forward an understanding of human civilization rooted in dialectical and historical materialism.

While the decaying Marxist-Leninist sect I was working with was attempting to recruit liberal activists, I began to notice and question the ineffectiveness of this strategy. This forced me to examine my own beliefs, my own motivations, and my own ideology, as well as the problems facing the entire leftist milieu in a new light.

Marxism is fundamentally optimistic

In "Critique of the Gotha Programme," Marx explained the material basis for the higher stage of communism, writing:

In a higher phase of communist society, after the enslaving subordination of the individual to the division of labor, and therewith also the antithesis between mental and physical labor, has vanished; after labor has become not only a means of life but life's prime want; after the productive forces have also increased with the all-around development of the individual, and all the springs of co-operative wealth flow more abundantly — only then can the narrow horizon of bourgeois right be crossed in its entirety and society inscribe on its banners: From each according to his ability, to each according to his needs![1]

In essence, Marx is explaining what historical materialism so brilliantly lays out in a way all other analysis cannot. Class society, social hierarchies, and the state itself are all rooted in scarcity. In a society without the all-around development of the individual, where the productive forces and technological progress of human beings is restrained by the irrationality of profits in command, much of the ugliness of the contemporary world becomes unavoidable.

However, Marxism argues that with central planning of the means of production, a post-scarcity society of vast abundance and egalitarianism can emerge. As Engels explained in *Socialism: Utopian and Scientific*:

Socialized production upon a predetermined plan becomes henceforth possible. The development of production makes the existence of different classes of society thenceforth an anachronism. In proportion as anarchy in social production vanishes, the political

---

1. Karl Marx, "Critique of the Gotha Programme" (1875), available online at https://www.marxists.org/archive/marx/works/1875/gotha/index.htm.

authority of the State dies out. Man, at last the master of his own form of social organization, becomes at the same time the lord over Nature, his own master — free.[2]

As Lenin explained: "Monopolies, oligarchy, the striving for domination and not for freedom, the exploitation of an increasing number of small or weak nations by a handful of the richest or most powerful nations — all these have given birth to those distinctive characteristics of imperialism which compel us to define it as parasitic or decaying capitalism."[3] The essence of Lenin's concept of imperialism as the highest state of capitalism is that development is being restrained. The world is being kept poor so the cartels of Wall Street and London finance, and in our age, the Malthusian social engineers of Silicon Valley can stay rich.

However, when countries have ripped free from the monopolistic domination of western cartels and reorganized their economies, huge successes have resulted. Socialism in the 20th century, despite the flaws and setbacks, demonstrated very clearly that it is capable of rapidly advancing technological progress and development. Russia was an agrarian, impoverished

---

2. Friedrich Engels, *Socialism: Utopian and Scientific* (1880), available online at https://www.marxists.org/archive/marx/works/1880/soc-utop/.

3. Vladimir Lenin, *Imperialism, the Highest Stage of Capitalism* (1916–17), available online at https://www.marxists.org/archive/lenin/works/1916/imp-hsc/.

society in 1917. With state central planning, mobilizing the country around five-year plans, overcoming the artificial restraints imposed by the market, the USSR wiped out illiteracy, fully electrified, defeated the Nazi invaders and conquered outer space. The first mobile phone was patented in the Soviet Union in 1957. Despite a NATO treaty barring the USSR from getting access to high technology, crippling economic warfare, and military threat, a home computer system was developed, and all kinds of amazing technological and scientific breakthroughs took place in Soviet society up into the 1980s.

Huawei Technologies, a state-controlled mega corporation created by the Chinese Communist Party, is the largest telecommunications manufacturer in the world, described by Harvard Business Review as a great example of successful profit-sharing.

With a Communist Party in power, state-run industries and banks, along with five-year plans and heavy control over the private sector, China has emerged to become the second largest economy in the world. With socialism China has built the largest telecommunications manufacturer, the largest steel industry, and the largest hydroelectric power plant in the world, as well as the fastest trains on the planet. Millions have been raised from poverty, access to education has vastly expanded, and technological achievements and breakthroughs are numerous.

Socialism created a healthcare system in Cuba which is admired all over the world for its achievements. Socialism in Bolivia created the highest GDP growth rates in South America consistently, while paving the roads and wiping out illiteracy. Quality modern housing has been brought to even the poorest Venezuelans. Nicaraguan socialism has eradicated illiteracy and enabled thousands of indigenous people to become micro-entrepreneurs.

With Socialism, Libya was the top oil-exporting country in Africa prior to 2011. It had the highest life expectancy according to the CIA World Factbook and it has constructed the world's largest irrigation system. No horror story of Gaddaffi's atrocities, alleged or truthful, can obscure this economic reality.

While capitalism and more recently, neoliberal economic reforms have left countries across Africa, Central America, and the Caribbean in crippling poverty, socialism turned Russia and China into industrial powerhouses and global superpowers. The endless browbeating of the claim "Socialism never worked! Communism completely failed!" is an effort to obscure, on the basis of human-rights violations, atrocities, and selectively highlighted episodes of mismanagement, the overall, obvious reality. Socialism works, and when countries break free from the imperialist global order, their economic achievements are significant.

This should be no surprise to those who study what Marx and Lenin actually wrote. However, if one listens to prevailing leftist voices in the western world, it can be highly confusing. The vision of a high-tech, post-scarcity world where human beings live out their full potential, what some have called a "resource-based economy," is largely now considered the property of libertarians and other elements who worship the profit motive. The spirit of growth and optimism observed in the Soviet Union by Anna Louise Strong, H.G. Wells, Sydney and Beatrice Webb, W.E.B. Dubois, Albert Einstein and so many other intellectuals is now associated with the Right wing and advocates of the free market.

Ideological Foundations of City-Building 9

Prior to being toppled by NATO bombs in 2011, the Islamic Socialist government of Libya constructed the world's largest irrigation system, the Great Man-Made River.

The economic strength of the Soviet Union as it rapidly industrialized inspired people across the planet, including many prominent intellectuals.

The "New Left" Was Fake

Meanwhile, many leftists now focus on the idea that capitalism is bad because it increases consumption. Capitalism is associated with "buying stuff" and "destroying the environment." Leftism is associated with "anti-consumerism" and the notion that the working people of the world should be poorer. Anti-imperialism has been consumed by a narrative best articulated in the Hollywood film *Avatar* (2009). David Brooks summed it up in the *New York Times* as "This is the oft-repeated story about a manly young adventurer who goes into the wilderness in search of thrills and profit. But, once there, he meets the native people and finds that they are noble and spiritual and pure. And so he emerges as their Messiah, leading them on a righteous crusade against his own rotten civilization."[4] In this new narrative that dominates leftism, imperialism is not bad because it holds back economic development, but because it brings it, tearing beautiful primitive peoples away from their spiritually pure ways.

The reason leftism has failed to capture the anger of the U.S. working class in a time of economic crisis is simple. Leftists no longer seek to improve their living conditions, but rather want to reduce them in the name of anti-consumerism and environmentalism. The reason leftists have been some of the most enthusiastic

---

4. David Brooks, "The Messiah Complex," *New York Times*, January 7, 2010.

supporters of regime-change wars and destabilization in Syria, Libya, Venezuela, Nicaragua, Russia, and China is because leftism no longer seeks to liberate the developing world from underdevelopment. Leftist narratives now celebrate the Dalai Lama, Wahhabi fanatics, the small minority of indigenous peoples in South and Central America who reject technology, and other groups deemed to be "noble savages" in the white savior fantasy of the ultra-rich. The enemy of such forces is of course the "authoritarian Marxist regimes" that build schools, hospitals, and power plants.

How on earth did anti-consumerism replace the struggle to raise productive forces and living standards with society rationally controlling the means of production? How on earth did the struggle to liberate the developing world from the monopolistic domination and forced poverty at the hands of western finance get replaced with notions similar to Mother Teresa's sickening mantra of "Poverty is Beautiful"?

The answer can be found in Lenin's analysis of the roots of social chauvinism, in the ideological confusion following the fall of the Soviet Union, one factor that cannot be overlooked is the direct intervention of the western intelligence apparatus. The Congress for Cultural Freedom program of the CIA is now a matter of public record. Nominally Left publications, such as *Partisan Review, Der Monat, Encounter, Paris Review*, and others were funded by the CIA along with the Ford and Rockefeller Foundations. They highlighted the work of Susan Sontag, Irving Howe, Hannah Arendt, Mary McCarthy, and others. They reinvented leftist thought to be an expression of middle-class alienation and pessimism that labels all populism as "fascist." The so-called "New Left" is a synthetic creation that accompanied the promotion of narcotics with Project MKULTRA, the utilization of various eastern religious cults as proxy forces, and various other criminal activities conducted by the U.S. intelligence agencies. The way U.S. culture was reinvented during the 1960s and 70s was not merely the result of

The CIA began manipulating leftist politics in 1949 with its Congress for Cultural Freedom program, funneling money to Trotskyites and other left anti-communists. The result has been a complete reinvention of the ideology.

progressive anti-racist struggles and opposition to Cold War conformity, but also the result of sinister efforts to confuse the public and lessen the danger of a real anti-capitalist movement emerging within the United States.

While it is an absolute taboo to discuss in leftist circles, these are facts any serious socialist in the U.S. must acknowledge. The infiltration, manipulation, subsidization of what calls itself "left-wing" in the United States has taken a huge ideological toll, and as a result socialism in the U.S. is in shambles as a few pieces of confused decaying Comintern wreckage scream at a much bigger layer of foundation-funded chaos worshippers and middle-class, academic, anti-social elements. The broad masses of working-class Americans see their living standards falling and are open to anti-capitalist notions, but they look at the destructive entity called "The Left" and want no part of it. They cannot be blamed or morally shamed for doing so.

Where do we go from here?

It may be tempting to become ideologically dogmatic and attempt to restore a more "pure" interpretation of Marxism in light of contemporary distortions, but this would also be a mistake. The Soviet Union collapsed because it could not effectively adjust its socialism in the way countries like Vietnam, Cuba, and China have. The 20th-century socialist countries often fell into the trap of attempting to build a totally egalitarian society in a state of underdevelopment and poverty, having disastrous consequences as seen in China's Cultural Revolution, Pol Pot's Democratic Kampuchea, and to a lesser degree in many other places.

The truth that Marx laid out in "Critique of the Gotha Programme" is that the entire basis of the communist project is unleashing human creativity and development. According to Engels, this is the very essence of human beings: "the animal merely *uses* its environment, and brings about changes in it simply by its presence; man by his changes makes it serve his ends, *masters* it. This is the final, essential distinction between man and other animals, and once again it is labour that brings about this distinction."[5]

The Center for Political Innovation is not a new Marxist party. Democratic Centralism in the United States has resulted in creating a number of irrelevant sects, none of which can truly call themselves a "party" in the sense of any force worthy of the label. The Center for Political Innovation does not seek to become the new "vanguard" or "leader of the movement." Rather, the Center for Political Innovation is an educational project aiming to get out of the movement and to the masses.

The goals are two-fold:

---

5. Friedrich Engels, "The Part Played by Labour in the Transition from Ape to Man," *Die Neue Zeit*, May–June 1876, available online at https://www.marxists.org/archive/marx/works/1876/part-played-labour/.

1. To propose a series of economic and political reforms that would challenge corporate power, and force those who support these demands into confrontation with the profit-centered economic system and its global dominance.

2. To teach genuine, constructive, anti-imperialist, optimistic, scientific socialism to all who want to learn it, facilitating debate and discussion among serious, professional worker-politicians about the concepts and ideology that can lead beyond capitalism and imperialism.

We should not be afraid to question aspects of Marxist theory in order to develop a socialism for our time. The anti-imperialist and socialist movements have changed a lot since the Cold War. Outside of

Non-Marxist forms of socialism that arose during the Cold War such as African Socialism, Baathist Arab Socialism, or the Islamic Socialism pioneered by Col. Moammar Gaddaffi in Libya should be actively studied by serious revolutionaries in the United States.

China, much of the socialist- and Marxist-led movements have embraced religious faith, most especially in Latin America. Baathism, socialism with Chinese characteristics, the anti-capitalism of Shia Muslims in the Middle East, African Socialism, and Bolivarianism all reinvented socialism for their own particular country and unique circumstances. Serious revolutionaries in the U.S. should be actively determining how this can be done here, and what will ultimately be the nature of a socialism with American characteristics.

Marx's ending to the *Communist Manifesto* contains the following instructions: "In short, the Communists everywhere support every revolutionary movement against the existing social and political order of things. In all these movements, they bring to the front, as the leading question in each, the property question, no matter what its degree of development at the time."[6]

Americans who are angry about losing their jobs, seeing their communities destroyed by opioids, their children locked up in prisons for profit, and their relatives sent off to die in foreign wars must be confronted with the property question. It should be made clear that instead of a weak corporate regime that presides over gradually collapsing the U.S. into just

---

6. Karl Marx and Friedrich Engels, *Manifesto of the Communist Party* (1847–48), available online at https://www.marxists.org/archive/marx/works/1848/communist-manifesto/index.htm.

another trading outpost for a global low-wage empire, another option exists.

The U.S. could instead have a government of action that fights for working families. Such a government would mobilize popular power and restructure the U.S. economy to serve public good, putting banking and natural resources under public ownership and management, while enacting an economic bill of rights for the population. It would see the population not as a dangerous mob to be managed but as a reservoir of potential to be unleashed toward building a post-scarcity world of abundance, freedom, and equality.

Amid the ideological confusion and increasing hopelessness of U.S. society, we consider ourselves to be representing the City-Building Tendency within the human species, and our roots go much deeper than Marx. Socrates, Confucius, Christ, Caesar, Spartacus and so many other courageous progressive individuals have given their lives to advancing humanity toward a higher state of being. We are an association of like-minded thinkers and dedicated agitators, cooperating in different ways in different communities across the country.

Those aligned with us deliver bottled water to impoverished families and the elderly in Texas, clean graveyards, operate within church congregations, on college campuses, in workplaces and neighborhoods. We distribute buttons that say "Cancel Student Debt" in NYC parks, conduct regular reading groups in Chicago and California, travel to anti-imperialist countries, appear on international television, hold debates with political opponents, publish books, and much more. Our goal is to help every participant in our project to discover what their own unique contribution can be when taking up history's challenge. We want you to fulfill your potential as a revolutionary, and our organizations exist, not to hold you back and glorify our leaders, but to unleash you to your highest possible achievement.

We reject Left adventurism and like all responsible revolutionary organizers we advocate a peaceful, democratic transition to socialism. We recognize that as capitalism enters a crisis, the ruling classes often move to abolish democratic rights in order to preserve their power. We recognize the people's right to defend their organizations and communities in such a context. However, we are absolutely clear that we want peace and stability, not chaos. It is capitalism that is destroying the United States of America, and socialism will rescue it, rebuilding the country on new foundations, overcoming the legacy of colonialism, slavery, and many other crimes that hang over this society as a curse.

The Center for Political Innovation, its youth organization Students and Youth for a New America, and its cadre outreach team the John Brown Volunteers are open to engaging with all who are willing to discuss and wrangle with how this important project can be carried out. It is in this spirit of open debate and seeking to forge groundbreaking discourse that this article has been submitted to the *Platypus Review*.

A CPI speakout in New York City's Central Park warning about the danger of a new world war in June of 2020.

The Masses Are the Water: Understanding the Failure of Late-Marcyism

The Party for Socialism and Liberation, Workers World Party, Struggle — La Lucha, the Communist Workers League and the New Orleans Workers Group all trace their roots back to the political brilliance of one man. However, his tactics and methods were not perfect and were specifically designed for a period very different from our own. It is urgent in our time for revolutionaries to get "Out of the Movement, To the Masses!"

The December 20th, 2021 issue of Struggle — La Lucha, the publication of one of Workers World Party's (WWP) many splinter groups contains the following tragic and almost comical headlines: "No support for Ukrainian Rittenhouses!" "Why there is no anti-vaccine movement in Cuba." On the anniversary of the January 6th Capitol Riot, Richard Becker, founding member of the Party for Socialism and Liberation (PSL) repeated the liberal claim that the events constituted an attempted coup during an appearance on PressTV. When challenged by Keaten Mansfield of the Center for Political Innovation, Becker went as far as saying that Mossad and Israel could not have possibly been involved in the day's events, despite the many Israeli flags displayed among Trump's crowd and Netanyahu's close alliance with the Trump White House.

While Jimmy Dore, Jackson Hinkle, Fred Hampton Leftists, members of the Communist Party USA, and supporters of the Center for Political Innovation participated in the "Medicare for All" marches across the country, the various organizational descendants of Sam Marcy have focused on protesting Trump as a "fascist," attempting to somehow lead the Black Lives Matter protests without inserting a class struggle message amid the identity politics, and otherwise taking their lead from CNN.

A Brilliant Organizer & Anti-Imperialist

Sam Marcy (1911-1998) was clearly a genius and brilliant Marxist organizer. His contribution to building anti-imperialist movements and class struggle in the post-WW2 years should be more widely studied in our time when even his own followers and ideological descendants work to obscure it. Samuel Ballan was born in Ukraine to a Jewish family and had vivid memories of the Red Army protecting his family during the Russian Civil War that followed the 1917 Bolshevik Revolution. Ballan migrated with his family to Brooklyn, New York, and as a teenager during the 1930s Great Depression, he joined the Communist Party USA and was heavily involved in its unemployed struggles and labor organizing. During this period the young activist took on the "party name" Sam Marcy after Marcy Avenue where he lived, and the pseudonym stuck for the rest of his life.

Sam Marcy resigned from the Communist Party USA and joined the Trotskyite movement at some

Sam Marcy founded Workers World Party in 1959 after being disgusted by the blatant anti-communism of the Trotskyite Socialist Workers Party.

point in 1933 or 1934. The reason he regularly stated for joining with Trotskyism and leaving the CPUSA was the failure of the Communist International to prevent Hitler's rise to power in Germany. However, there may have been other, more personal, factors. Later in his life, Marcy often castigated the CPUSA for attempting to appear "more American" by elevating US-born white men like William Z. Foster, Earl Browder, and Gus Hall to leadership positions in order to combat the perception that they were foreign agents. It is very likely that as a Jewish Ukrainian immigrant who grew up speaking Russian, the policy of attempting to "Americanize" the party's image directly impacted him in a negative way.

Marcy is known to have spoken harshly about the decision to move CPUSA's national headquarters to Chicago in 1928. William Z. Foster's position that this industrial city should be the capital of a "Soviet America" was considered by Marcy to be pandering to reaction. He maintained a kind of Atlanticist perception of the country, with a subtle contempt and suspicion of the broad masses of working people, perhaps rooted in his family's direct experience of horrendous persecution at the hands of European Christians, and certainly reinforced by the reactionary turn of US society in the post-war years. Like Trotsky, Marcy believed New York City was the "foundry where the fate of mankind will be forged," and this mindset was a barrier to reaching the broad masses of Americans.

Rejecting "Vulgar Anti-Stalinism"

Marcy joined the Trotskyites, but found himself increasingly uncomfortable with the anti-communism and middle-class nature of these circles. Many of the "New York Intellectuals" who dominated Trotskyism in the city during the late 1930s eventually abandoned Trotskyism for Neo-Conservatism. The most prominent of the New York City Trotskyites was Max Shachtman who broke with Trotsky in 1939, claiming the Molotov-Ribbentrop Pact proved the USSR could not be a "degenerated workers state."

Max Shachtman, the leader of the "New York Intellectuals" who dominated Trotskyism in the city ultimately broke with Trotsky in 1939. Many of his followers became Neocons.

Marcy, along with a few allies such as Vince Copeland (step-father of WWP leader Deirdre Griswold), relocated to the industrial city of Buffalo near the Canadian border. Marcy formed his own branch of the Socialist Workers Party, and amid McCarthyism, the Buffalo branch of the SWP was known for its lack of hostility to the CPUSA. While many Trotskyites celebrated the repression of the CPUSA, Sam Marcy and his disciples teamed up with the CPUSA to protest against Taft-Hartley, in support of the Rosenbergs, and for Civil Rights.

In 1956, Marcy saw Khrushchev's secret speech in a negative light, rather than as validation of Trotsky's criticism of Stalin. Marcy also saw the Hungarian Revolt of 1956 as a counter-revolutionary fascist uprising and defended the Soviet Union's intervention. Marcy wrote a number of documents critiquing the "vulgar anti-Stalinism" of the Trotskyites. By 1959 it became clear that Marcy's "Global Class War Tendency" was at odds with the rest of the Socialist Workers Party and a new party with a new newspaper was formed. The name "Workers World Party" was not chosen until a year after the initial split according to some records.

After leaving the SWP, Marcy pointed to Black Nationalism at home and Mao Zedong, Fidel Castro, and the postwar wave of third world revolutionary movements abroad as the center of revolutionary energy. While Marcy still considered his grouping to be the purest interpreters of Trotsky's teaching, after the early 1960s, WWP rarely quoted or promoted Trotsky in a public way. While internally considering themselves to be in line with Trotsky's Theory of Permanent Revolution, WWP realized that Trotskyism was becoming rightly synonymous with counter-revolution and middle-class anti-communism. Marcy developed his own criticism of Trotsky's organizing style, and by the 1970s, WWP's ideology was a complete ideological mish-mash centered around one great leader with license to interpret revolutionary theory.

WWP aligned itself with all Marxist-Leninist governments, not falling into the divisions of the Sino-Soviet Split, and recruited many young street fighting activists during the political upsurge of 1968-1972. Marcy's success as an economic forecaster and geopolitical analyst won him the respect of Fidel Castro and Kim Il-Sung, both of whom personally sat down

Sam Marcy meets with Fidel Castro in October, 1993.

with him on multiple occasions. Marcy analyzed events like the Chinese Cultural Revolution, the Kampuchea War, and the rise of Euro-Communism with a level of perception and depth rarely found elsewhere among western Marxists.

"Face to the Masses"

By 1974, Marcy had built up a cadre of nearly a thousand followers, most of them teenagers and college-aged radicals. When it became clear that upheavals of the early 70s had ended, Marcy oriented his followers to build community organizations focused on economic issues such as jobs, rent, food prices, and veterans benefits. The Marcyites organized a very successful demonstration against the racist anti-busing riots in Boston.

This post-1960s turn was labelled "face to the masses." The Center for United Labor Action was envisioned to be something like the CPUSA's Trade Union Educational League of the 1920s, and while economic populist and anti-racist activism kept the membership very busy, WWP adopted the practice of concealing itself. The feeling was that average workers were not intelligent enough to understand the sophisticated Marxism Marcy taught, and that anti-communism necessitated organizing a semi-underground organization to covertly lead pro-labor and anti-racist protests. WWP's idea of being "mass" or "popular" was headlines about unemployment or bemoaning food prices. The elitist perception that average Americans were just too stupid to understand Marxism-Leninism and could only be "agitated" and manipulated by economist rhetoric prevented WWP from recruiting or expanding its ranks. Most of WWP's recruits came from either the middle-class street mobilizations of the 60s, or from other wings of the Marxist movement during the various regroupments amid the confusion of 1970s and the New Communist Movement.

As the Socialist Workers Party declined in the late 70s, Workers World Party stepped up to fill the void by becoming the primary organizer of national anti-war protests in Washington DC. In May of 1981, WWP organized a massive demonstration called "The People's Anti-War Mobilization." This was the first national anti-war protest to have a Palestinian speaker and an LGBT speaker. In the following years, loyal Marcyite underlings Brian Becker, Richard Becker, and Gloria La Riva learned the art of outmaneuvering political rivals for permits and utilizing their leverage as "King of the Protest Cage" in the decades to come.

As the 1980s and 90s went on, Marcy oriented his followers to "take over the movement" and dominate left-wing spaces where veterans of the 1960s upsurge congregated and regrouped. The way protests in Washington DC are regulated, securing a permit enables an organization to have a state sanctioned monopoly on a public space for a certain period of time. WWP's rivals became infuriated with the sectarian nature with which the organization claimed its "turf" with the authority of the capitalist government. WWP employed a team of marshals to cooperate with the police and remove anyone who challenged Brian Becker's "face time" in international media or narcissistic rambling before introducing each scheduled speaker.

WWP convened the "All People's Congress" in Detroit and held national progressive demonstrations on an almost annual basis. The rallies grew to have a more and more liberal nature as time went by, though

Workers World Party organized a massive protest in 1981 called The People's Anti-War Mobilization. The party concealed its ideology in order to appeal to liberals. It was the first of many national protests called by WWP in Washington DC.

the Marcyites were always careful to include the demands of every anti-imperialist struggle from Palestine to the Philippines in the fine print of posters promoting demonstrations with names like "We Won't Take Four More Years!" or "The People's March Against Reaganism!"

The reason WWP had substantial success with "taking over the movement" during this period was because leftism was in decline and imperialism was stabilizing. The imperialists had no need to foment social democracy to control the discontented masses or mobilize a "movement" of foot soldiers in bonapartist struggles within the ruling class. When "the movement" existed as a kind of leftover from the 1960s upsurge, a group of disciplined, hardline Marxist-Leninist cadre could effectively maneuver into leadership of it.

In the age of BreadTube, Jacobin, and well-funded and widely promoted social-imperialist trends, the opposite is the case.

He Had No Crystal Ball

Sam Marcy was known to say "I have no crystal ball" as a kind of disclaimer before making his often correct economic forecasts. The phrase was meant to emphasize that Marxism was a science based on understanding the objective laws of history, not a form of mystical divination. The fact that Marcy had no crystal ball became very apparent in 1989-1993 when Marcy was completely blindsided by the fall of the Soviet Union and the Eastern Bloc. Marcy had oriented his followers to operate as if no such thing could ever occur. With tragic optimism up into 1992 and 1993 Marcy continued to insist that "it's not over yet" and that there was still hope for the Soviet Union to be revived.

The reason that Sam Marcy and his followers had been blindsided by the fall of the USSR was because they had taken tactical direction from it. They had focused on opposing the military industrial complex and Republicans as the main danger to the USSR, building up the anti-nuclear movement and protests against "Reaganism." In his book "The Bolsheviks and War" Marcy called for the anti-war movement to "take on a working-class character." He wrote: "These giant multi-national monopolies are more powerful than any ancient empire ever was. There are even few modern imperialist states that can rival the power of one of the dynastic finance capitalist groupings which bankroll the various weapons systems. They relentlessly milk the U.S. Treasury which in turn passes on its losses to the masses of the working class and oppressed. If the struggle against imperialist war is to become serious, it must take on a working-class character. That doesn't mean to narrow the appeal, as capitalist politicians maintain. On the contrary, it means to broaden it, for it is the working class and the oppressed people together with the lower middle class that constitute the majority in any case. Taking on a working-class character means that the fundamental aim of the anti-war struggle is not merely against the military-industrial complex, but also the defense contractors and the big banks, as well as the giant oil corporations. In a word, the struggle against imperialist war must be conducted as an all-around class wide struggle against the bourgeoisie."

What Marcy failed to recognize is that in addition to the Reagans, Bushes and Pentagon Brass, the

The Soviet Union believed the military industrial complex was the primary threat they faced. They oriented their allies to embed themselves in liberal and pacifist activism.

bourgeoisie had a liberal side well-embedded in the intelligence apparatus. Intelligence-connected occult guru Marilyn Ferguson who served as Al Gore's spiritual advisor, the Congress for Cultural Freedom program of the CIA, the MKULTRA drug and mind control operations all worked to bring down the Soviet Union by more covert means.

While the military industrial complex had most certainly been threatened by the lack of hawkishness within the Carter administration as Marcy observed in his book *Generals Over the White House*, Carter was not simply a two-faced liberal appeaser of the masses. Marcy noted that events following the 1979 Iranian Revolution in the lead up to the 1980 election represented an internal conflict among the bourgeoisie.

Zbigniew Brzezinski, Jimmy Carter's national security advisor, developed a strategy of manipulating communists against each other. It was these kind of liberal covert operations and psyops that ultimately defeated the USSR, not military threat.

He wrote: "There are contradictions in the imperialist camp, as evidenced by the unwillingness of the imperialist allies to support the U.S. military adventure in Iran, or to go whole-hog with Washington in its confrontational brinkmanship with the USSR... Most significant is the inability of the Carter administration to get the kind of response from the mass of the American people that it needs in order to really launch a war. And this is despite having pulled out all the stops in a flood of jingoistic and chauvinist propaganda that has saturated the masses. It is no longer the early 1950s or even the 1960s when there was capitalist economic stability and development. The U.S. capitalist economy has now been in decline for several years, wracked by galloping inflation and rising unemployment."

What Marcy missed was that while National Security Advisor Zbigniew Brzezinski may have left the White House with Carter, the soft-power manipulative strategies he advocated and the Rockefeller think tanks that dreamed them up remained intact. The antinuclear movement of the 1980s, the inflow of liberal intellectuals to the USSR in the same decade, the covert funding of Marxian academics in Europe, and the courting and manipulation of dissident intellectuals in the Eastern Bloc all continued.

The USSR was not brought down by military threat, but from ideological penetration. The cultural hedonism and pessimistic thinking of the New Left, spawned by US intelligence agencies, had seeped into

The manipulation of young intellectuals in the Eastern Bloc by US intelligence was key in staging uprisings like the Prague Spring in 1968, and eventually the various Color Revolutions that overturned socialism.

the Soviet intelligentsia and boosted the Gorbachev wing of the Soviet leadership. "Democratic Socialism" and "anti-Stalinism" had wooed many among the younger generation of Soviet Communists into having a less hostile view of US imperialism and denouncing the "dogmatism" of their forefathers. The cultivation of dissident elements during the 1970s and 80s in the Eastern Bloc involved a large number of people being sucked into the delusion that they were part of a "global consciousness raising movement" that is "neither pro-communist or anti-communist" but seeks to "bring people together" and spread "open-mindedness and freedom." The strategies of Zbigniew Brzezinski were carried out with covert projects often funded by Hungarian Billionaire George Soros, creating ideological confusion in Soviet society and paving the way for Yeltsin among a population weary of war and economic embargoes.

The "New Left" that Marcy's followers embedded themselves in and pandered to while often concealing their own politics ultimately delivered the "stab in the back" that destroyed the USSR. There's a reason that Fidel Castro condemned rock music and drugs and other socialist states viewed counterculture with open contempt. The Marcyite tendency overlooked the illiberalism of socialist states and tragically underestimated the importance of ideological and cultural struggle. The New Left should have been treated as a serious ideological threat, not a useful milieu to be courted and maneuvered within. "Movementism" or "Movementarian Revisionism" can correctly be identified as the greatest flaw of the Marcyite tendency.

Amid the string of bitter defeats, Marcy composed a pamphlet called "Soviet Socialism: Utopian or Scientific" in 1992 falling back on the Trotskyite theory of Permanent Revolution, insisting that the Soviet Union was doomed from the beginning because no workers' revolution had happened in the west, and it existed in competition with capitalist powers. Marcy wrote:

"Why did it [the Utopian commune of New Harmony] disintegrate? The common explanation given by bourgeois critics of these early communist experiments is that they failed to reward "personal initiative" and the "rugged individualism" for which capitalist imperialism is so famous. However, the more important reason for their failure was that they were in competition with the capitalist mode of production and dependent upon it for the purchase and sale of materials. Even the Rappites who were quite prosperous, had had to move their communal society from Indiana to Pittsburgh to be nearer the market... Communism as an idea has existed for centuries. Communist societies like New Harmony and New Lanark and hundreds of others were not an accident of history but a response to the meanness, inequality, poverty, etc., of class society... Now that the counterrevolution is fully in the saddle in the USSR, and its wrecking crews are breaking down every progressive and revolutionary reform shall we say that this too was a form of utopianism? Was not the Soviet Union in reality as isolated as was New Harmony? Was it not an attempt to build an oasis within a world imperialist environment that was rent by malignant class contradictions?... **The socialist revolution unexpectedly broke out first in Russia, not in an advanced capitalist country. The USSR was to a large extent an isolated phenomenon in a world still dominated by capitalism. Although it covered one-sixth of the earth's surface, it was surrounded by a world imperialist environment. The Bolsheviks had a revolutionary and scientific approach to building socialism but they were no more immune to the social environment, to the domination of monopoly capitalism on a world scale, than was New Harmony in its day.**" [Emphasis from C.M.]

Trotsky's Theory of Permanent Revolution is predicated on the assumption that the western capitalist countries will always be the center of the world economy. Trotsky and Sam Marcy both failed to foresee that Russia and China would continue rising while the west deteriorated into a capitalist crisis.

What Marcy (and Trotsky) failed to predict was that by the first decade of the 21st Century the world would be on a steady trajectory of no longer being centered around the west. Socialist revolutions laid the basis for Russia and China to emerge as superpowers and fill the void as western capitalism became more unstable as a result of the computer revolution. The USA is on the brink of societal collapse, not social revolution, and if such a collapse happens the globe can easily re-center itself around the two Eurasian superpowers that are already supplying the world with the majority of its telecommunications technology, computer chips, steel, oil and natural gas. The idea that the peoples of the world are stuck "waiting for the workers in America to move" is a 20th century delusion excessively repeated in Marcyite workshops. The face of geopolitics has changed.

The Becker Family Walks Away

Learning nothing from the disastrous fall of the USSR, WWP focused on "building the movement" and embracing the pessimistic, drug infested, sex obsessed middle class trend that dominates leftist spaces in the United States even more in the 1990s. WWP was ahead of its time in a way, with the kind of cancel culture, bitter punitive atmosphere and identity politics obsession that is now typical in almost any "socialist" environment first being unleashed inside the Manhattan loft of the International Action Center. WWP never recruited a substantial amount of people of color, and was always a primarily white organization. However, in the name of aspiring to be the vanguard of the Black liberation struggle certain individuals were given veto power over anything the organization did and protected from any criticism of their actions.

Brian Becker's skills as a protest stage manager came in handy in 2002-2004 during the height of protests against the Iraq War. Seeing an opportunity, the ANSWER (Act Now Stop War End Racism) coalition was formed and began reserving protest permits. With enough money coming in and a layer of cadre loyal to him and the ANSWER coalition rather than the party overall, the Becker family led more than half of WWP to walk away and form the Party for Socialism and Liberation in 2004.

IDEOLOGICAL FOUNDATIONS OF CITY-BUILDING   41

Brian Becker formed the ANSWER coalition and eventually walked away from Workers World Party to form the Party for Socialism and Liberation (PSL) with his brother Richard Becker, and sister-in-law Gloria La Riva. Brian Becker's son Ben Becker is the editor of PSL's print newspaper.

WWP responded to the split by accusing PSL of being "racist" and re-energizing for a bit. Fred Goldstein, one of Marcy's older proteges who had mentored Brian, composed a book called "Low Wage Capitalism" giving a Marxist perspective on the financial crisis and started acting as WWP's new theoretician. A slew of ex-members who had been driven out amid the group's decay in the 1990s were welcomed back as long as they denounced Brian Becker as a traitor to Marcy's legacy. Fred Goldstein oriented the party to once again emphasize economic demands and highlight the history of the CPUSA's role during the 1930s. From 2008 to 2011 the organization seemed to have some aspiration to be a functional, class struggle anti-imperialist organization like the Communist Party of Greece (KKE) or other more healthy Marxist-Leninist groups around the world.

But even amid its brief resurgence, the seeds of failure and collapse had already been planted. In 2008 WWP cadre were oriented to not criticize Barack Obama and to celebrate his election as a huge victory over racism. During the 2011 Occupy protests, WWP cadre proved completely incapable of answering basic ideological questions young activists presented them or winning over any substantial layer of the many young people interested in anti-capitalist ideas. At this point it became clear that "The movement" was run by somebody else, who believed something very different. The 1980s and 90s were over and the ruling class was fomenting Synthetic Leftism for its own reasons. WWP was not going to be able to "take over" Occupy Wall Street or Black Lives Matter, especially when it did not even understand its own ideology.

In 2012, with a slick package of NGO money traceable to the very banks they were protesting, WWP stage managed the protests against the Democratic National Convention in Charlotte, North Carolina. The protests were held the day prior to the convention and instead of exposing the Democrats, they called a "March on Wall

Street South" that barely criticized the White House.

While WWP endorsed Cynthia McKinney's Green Party campaign in 2008, in 2012 the party was completely silent, giving almost a passive endorsement to Obama. In 2016 Monica Moorhead ran an embarrassing identity politics laced campaign, echoing MSNBC's claims that Trump was a fascist while the party pathetically attempted to lead liberal anti-Trump mobilizations. In January of 2017 while Trump was being sworn in, WWP held a small demonstration along with the Freedom Road Socialist Organization. The feeder march eventually merged into the liberal crowd who carried signs accusing Trump of being a Russian asset and comparing him to Kim Jong-Un.

While "Tankie" politics becomes increasingly relevant in the current climate of ideological confusion, Marcyism and its failed movementist strategy is certainly in decline. Brian Becker's Party for Socialism and Liberation is the largest and most effective piece of Marcyite Cold War wreckage, though many of its younger members do not even know Marcy's name. Following the Marcyite tradition, PSL stages rallies around the latest trendy liberal causes, hoping fruitlessly to convince crowds that think Trump is a Russian agent to oppose regime change wars.

For the anniversary of the January 6th Capitol Riot, PSL's *Liberation* republished a transcript of Brian Becker's rather unoriginal rambling about the events saying "When one examines January 6, what Trump tried to do was prevent the peaceful transfer of power from one ruling class party to the other. This is a cornerstone of the legitimacy, or perceived legitimacy, of the American system of governance — the fact that when one side loses the election, it doesn't, you know, end up in street fighting or civil war, which would be the hallmark of an unstable system of governance. The US has acknowledged this peaceful transition, at least since the end of the civil war in 1865. So what Trump did is he violated this basic rule — the cardinal rule of politics in America — by putting his own interests ahead of the interests of the capitalist system to demonstrate stability in its form of governance… I think the most important failure of the Democratic party was the way they did not encourage the prosecution of the chief architects of the violent assault, meaning they did not file charges against Trump and his entourage who clearly planned this event. They were the ones who summoned tens of thousands of Trump supporters to Washington in the middle of the work week."

One almost wonders if Becker is hoping his "Socialist Program" podcast will be picked up by MSNBC. The notion that the Democratic Party which is embracing tech censorship, cancel culture, sweeping "domestic terrorism" legislation, and all kinds of political repression in the aftermath of the Capitol Riot is somehow not going far enough is a bizarre thing for any supposed Marxist revolutionary to say.

PSL has called for heavy handed repression of Trump supporters, accusing them of "sedition." The Sedition Act of 1918 was used to suppress socialist anti-war speech during the First World War.

Perhaps the ANSWER coalition will next hold rallies in Washington DC calling for the mass confiscation of firearms or placing "Russian Assets" in concentration camps to protect the homeland? As working people are being driven deeper into poverty amid post-pandemic inflation, with war danger rising as US media is whipping up cultural divisions, PSL's "great achievement" is holding rallies in the hopes of helping to drive Kyle Rittenhouse out of Arizona State University.

In multiple instances Becker has used the term "sedition" to describe the rowdy demonstration of Trump supporters that involved trespassing and vandalism. One wonders if Becker is not familiar with *Schenck v. United States* or *Abrams v. United States*. The 1918 Sedition Act was created specifically to silence socialist anti-war protesters like him. But now that Becker is simply defending the liberal order from dissident rightists, his concern for civil liberties has vanished.

Youth who attend PSL functions and show a knowledge of or strong interest in Marxism will be treated with suspicion. PSL Cadre are quick to tell you "We are real organizers! We aren't interested in those books by old white men!" PSL wants to be a protest club for young liberal hipsters, not a group of working people embracing history's challenge. If one challenges PSL's ideological positions or tactics, the argument will inevitably lead to the classic Marcyite-movementist refrain of "Yeah? Well we actually do something!" PSL recruitment materials, while slicker and having better production values than other socialist tendencies, are about as watered down and liberal as you can get. Recruitment videos consist of members staring into a camera saying something more or less equivalent to "Look at us! We are a group of people of diverse races and genders who can recite liberal mantras! Don't you think racism and war are bad? Join the PSL because we do lots of protesting and stuff."

The fact that PSL nominated Gloria La Riva as their 2020 Presidential candidate instead of a younger or more charismatic cadre reveals an entrenched bureaucratism that will ultimately doom the organization beyond its mistaken tactical orientation. PSL is the property of the Becker family and their selected clique of activists, a protest hustle they have opportunistically monetized and will never willingly give up despite the actual needs of the class struggle. Like WWP, PSL will cling to the toxic liberal "movement" and continue to reassure everyone of its supposed potential, much like musicians who kept strumming away as the Titanic sank.

"The Movement is Everything! The Goal is Nothing!"

In 2017 and 2018 Workers World Party fractured, first with a hysterical purge against the Detroit branch for daring to challenge Marcy's handpicked lifelong successors, followed by sexual assault scandals, rape allegations and violence between members resulting from events in Baltimore. The party is now roughly a third of the size it was in 2015, with a few ever-loyal cadre holding on and a few naive youth who will most likely see through the scam in a year or two. A couple more sincere breakaway splinter groups made up of old believers repeating Sam Marcy's Cold War mantras have websites and newspapers, while what's left of the party itself functions as an undead animated corpse staging small rallies and maintaining a very expensive but almost always empty office in midtown Manhattan.

Many figures formerly associated with WWP such as Imani Henry and Elena Everett have devolved into mere liberal activists, taking WWP's disdain for ideology and celebration of liberal activism to its logical conclusion. Former WWP cadre Taryn Fivek has moved on to the CPUSA, where she and a small clique of well-connected allies are whipping up a hysterical campaign against the Center for Political Innovation that much of the party's rank and file is highly uncomfortable with. Fivek's theatrics center around the conspiracy theory that Russian intellectual Alexander Dugin is covertly directing Jimmy Dore, Glenn Greenwald and this writer in a sinister plot to undermine Joe Biden's progressive agenda and Kamala Harris' reputation.

Edward Bernstein's slogan "The Movement is Everything! The Goal is Nothing!" with which he coined the term 'revisionism' would most likely be met with approval by most late Marcyites if a poll were taken. Such thinking is far more dangerous in 2022 than in 1910.

Millions of Americans do not trust the government, the Pentagon, big pharma or the mainstream media. In the hopes of drumming up some public support and beating back the dissident right-wing, US imperialism is attempting to have a "woke" makeover. Rather than winning the working class away from Trumpian demagogy in a time when they are more critical of the status quo than ever before, the Marcyites have instead opted to join "the movement" fomented by the imperialists in the hope of saving their system.

The notion that PSL, WWP or some other Marxist organization will be permitted by the bourgeoisie to maneuver into leadership of their mobilizations to defend the status quo against Trump is pure delusion. The Popular Front alliance of the Roosevelt-era was only possible because the Communist Party had spent the previous half-decade building up a huge base of support among impoverished urban workers. At the time, the Communist Party USA was tied to the Soviet Union and Roosevelt aligning with it also had geopolitical implications amid the imperialist rivalry with Germany and Italy.

Trump is not Hitler. The USA is not Weimar Germany. Furthermore, the crowds of middle-class CNN college liberals being mobilized to defend the wildly unpopular Biden administration do not represent the proletariat. The BreadTube/Young Turks/DSA cult that mesmerizes its recruits with infantalizing corporate-style "Wokeshops" rooted in scientology practices, while calling for concentration camps for the unvaccinated and equating "Tankies" with Nazi holocaust deniers, is not where serious revolutionaries should be attempting to recruit. While conservatives and right-wing dissidents often appear open to conversation despite their backward views, the vile, hateful entity called "the movement" looks a lot more like fascism to those who understand what the term actually means.

Socialist Heroism: "Lower and Deeper, to the Real Masses"

Socialism is the only way out of the unfolding nightmare of US capitalism. The teachings of the proletarian movement and its message of salvation, comradeship, and emancipation must become well embedded among the broad masses of Americans. Imperialism is the enemy of American workers and the greatest cure for racism has always been the picket line, bringing working people together to see their common interest against the bankers and warmakers. To be truly patriotic and love the United States, to truly follow the teachings of Jesus Christ, it is necessary to embrace anti-imperialism and socialism.

The above sentiments must be made abundantly clear to millions of people. This is the **urgent necessity** of the moment. The Marcyites will never take on this task because deep down they do not love the broad masses. Much like Hillary Clinton who dismissed all of Trump's supporters as a "basket of deplorables," the late Marcyites view average American working people who aren't as "woke" as they are with contempt.

During the Cold War, it certainly made sense for Communists to retreat into the labor movement or hippie counterculture as the comfortable lifestyle of many US workers was a basis for the chauvinism, racism and anti-communism among a big layer of the country.

But the Cold War is long over, and the labor aristocracy is being eroded. Living standards are falling. The Center for Political Innovation seeks to reorient socialism away from the New Left's distortions. Demands for jobs, housing, and schools have potential to take hold among the broad masses, as do anti-imperialist sentiments. However, in order to reach the broad masses, a solid break with the toxic, middle class, pro-imperialist "woke" left and its liberal cultural atmosphere must take place.

Lenin wrote: "Neither we nor anyone else can calculate precisely what portion of the proletariat is following and will follow the social-chauvinists and opportunists. This will be revealed only by the struggle, it will be definitely decided only by the socialist revolution. But we know for certain that the "defenders of the fatherland" in the imperialist war represent only a minority. And it is therefore our duty, if we wish to remain socialists, to go down lower and deeper, to the real masses; this is the whole meaning and the whole purport of the struggle against opportunism. By exposing the fact that the opportunists and social-chauvinists are in reality betraying and selling the interests of the masses, that they are defending the temporary privileges of a minority of the workers, that they are the vehicles of bourgeois ideas and influences, that they are really allies and agents of the bourgeoisie, we teach the masses to appreciate their true political interests, to fight for socialism and for the revolution through all the long and painful vicissitudes of imperialist wars and imperialist armistices."

The question facing US society is whether or not it will be restructured with socialism and join the alternative global economy, or simply deteriorate along with the Atlanticist international system. Rosa Luxemburg's question of "socialism or barbarism?" raised in 1915 amid the First World War has returned with a vengeance. Luxemburg wrote: "Today, we face the choice exactly as Friedrich Engels foresaw it a generation ago: either the triumph of imperialism and the collapse of all civilization as in ancient Rome, depopulation, desolation, degeneration — a great cemetery. Or the victory of socialism, that means the conscious active struggle of the international proletariat against imperialism and its method of war."

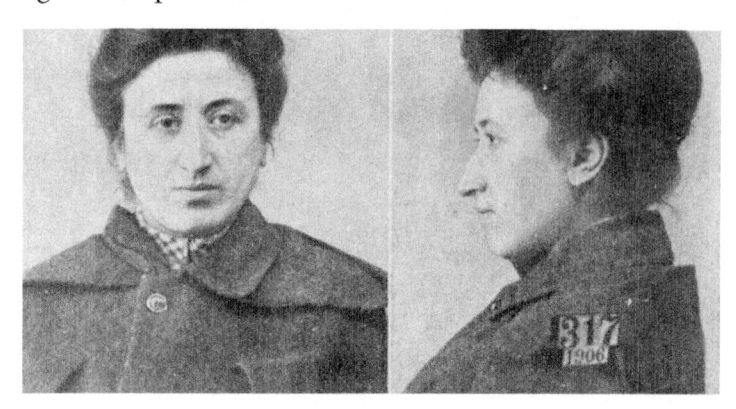

Rosa Luxemburg, locked up in Germany for her anti-war activism, argued that imperialism would ultimately lead to the western capitalist countries collapsing into barbarism much like the Roman Empire.

In such a time the goal of leftists cannot be to simply "burn it down" and spread chaos within the USA in solidarity with the third world. A program for stabilizing US society by breaking it out of the international monopolist system and transitioning to a rational socialist economy must be put forward. Socialists must be the political current that offers the working people of America hope for progress, peace, stability, and community in the face of chaotic imperialist societal collapse.

The reason Stalin ascended into leadership of the Soviet Communist Party was because unlike Trotsky, he had a deep love and spiritual connection with the peoples of the region. Stalin was not a cosmopolitan intellectual of the revolutionary intelligentsia, but the son of a boot-maker who grew up in a small village. Prior to 1917 Stalin, himself a Georgian, organized factory workers, peasants, and workers of many different ethnic and religious backgrounds into a unified disciplined organization. In his biography of Stalin, British historian Simon Sebag Montefiore described his methods: "Stalin was hostile to bumptious intellectuals, but he was less with the less educated worker-revolutionaries, who did not arouse his inferiority complex, he played the teacher — the priest… The workers listened reverently to this young preacher — and it was no coincidence that many of the revolutionaries were seminarists, and the workers often pious ex-peasants… Trotsky, agitating in another

The effectiveness of Stalin in leading the Soviet peoples to rapidly industrialize and defeat the Nazis came from a deep love and spiritual connection with the population.

city, remembered that many of the workers thought the movement resembled the early Christians and had to be taught that they should be atheists."

Stalin's effectiveness in mobilizing the USSR to rapidly industrialize and defeat the Nazis came from being amazingly in touch with the soul of the Soviet peoples. He understood what compromises to make, what methods of persuasion to use, and how to build the Soviet state into an effective vehicle for transforming and defending the land. US Communists must strive to have this deep love and connection with the various peoples of the United States, Black, Arab, Asian, Latino and white, Christian, Muslim, Jewish, Hindu, men, women, or LGBT. Beyond Wall Street and Hollywood, between Canada and Mexico, there is a huge country full of working families, vast natural resources, and a hopeful optimism that once gave US society a special glow and energy amid the rightly decried ugliness of its history. Mao Zedong wrote: "The masses are the water, and the revolutionaries are the fish."

The strategy of mass socialist education among the wider population, summed up by the slogan "Out of the Movement, To the Masses!" is the only option for serious anti-imperialists.

Marcy's late cold war strategies and analysis contain many important lessons, but as its ideological heirs become weaker and more attached to the liberals, the "movementist" approach must be chucked.

In a time where millions of working-class youth feel disempowered and hopeless, the City-Building Tendency must appeal to their inner desire to become heroic. In his pivotal text "The Role of the Individual in History," Georgi Plekhanov the father of Russian Marxism wrote: "A great man is precisely a beginner because he sees further than others, and desires things more strongly than others… He is a hero. But he is not a hero in the sense that he can stop, or change, the natural course of things, but in the sense that his activities are the conscious and free expression of this inevitable and unconscious course. Herein lies all his significance; herein lies his whole power. But this significance is colossal, and the power is terrible."

Printed in Great Britain
by Amazon